You can find butterflies
on cold mountains...

and in hot deserts.

Butterflies are insects
like flies and ladybugs.
They have six legs,
a body in three parts,
and skin that is hard like a shell.
Like most insects,
butterflies have wings.

Put Beginning Readers on the Right Track with
ALL ABOARD READING™

The All Aboard Reading series is especially for beginning readers. Written by noted authors and illustrated in full color, these are books that children really and truly *want* to read—books to excite their imagination, tickle their funny bone, expand their interests, and support their feelings. With four different reading levels, All Aboard Reading lets you choose which books are most appropriate for your children and their growing abilities.

Picture Readers—for Ages 3 to 6
Picture Readers have super-simple texts, with many nouns appearing as rebus pictures. At the end of each book are 24 flash cards—on one side is the rebus picture; on the other side is the written-out word.

Level 1—for Preschool through First-Grade Children
Level 1 books have very few lines per page, very large type, easy words, lots of repetition, and pictures with visual "cues" to help children figure out the words on the page.

Level 2—for First-Grade to Third-Grade Children
Level 2 books are printed in slightly smaller type than Level 1 books. The stories are more complex, but there is still lots of repetition in the text, and many pictures. The sentences are quite simple and are broken up into short lines to make reading easier.

Level 3—for Second-Grade through Third-Grade Children
Level 3 books have considerably longer texts, harder words, and more complicated sentences.

All Aboard for happy reading!

For Mom and Dad—E.B.N.

In memory of Katelyn Webb.
We will forever cherish that special closeness,
and the cuddles shared while reading books
together—Love, Mom & Dad

ISBN 0-439-26438-3

12 11 10 9 8 7   04 03

Printed in the U.S.A.   23

First Scholastic printing, March 2001

ALL
ABOARD
READING™

Level 1
Preschool-Grade 1

Butterflies

By Emily Neye
Illustrated by Ron Broda

SCHOLASTIC INC.
New York Toronto London Auckland Sydney
Mexico City New Delhi Hong Kong

Butterflies live
all over the world.
They are in backyard gardens.

They are in
rainforests far away.

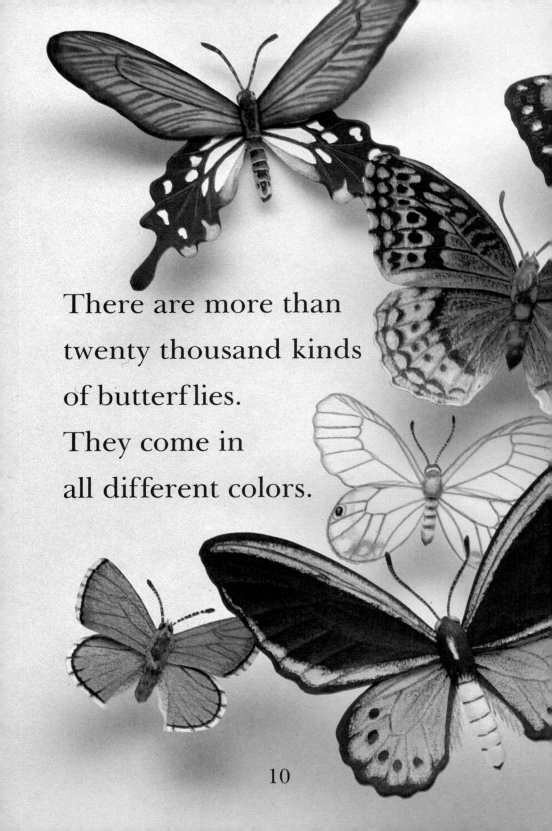

There are more than
twenty thousand kinds
of butterflies.
They come in
all different colors.

Butterflies come
in different sizes.
The biggest butterfly has wings
as wide as a robin's wings.

The smallest butterfly
is about the size
of this picture.

But every butterfly
starts out the same way—
as a tiny egg.

This monarch butterfly
(you say it like this: MON-ark)
has just laid
one of her eggs on a leaf.

egg

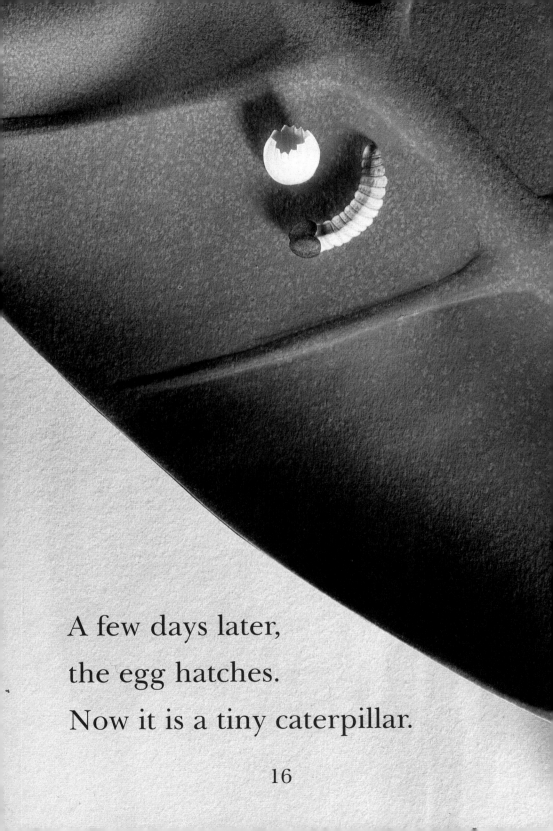

A few days later,
the egg hatches.
Now it is a tiny caterpillar.

All the caterpillar does is
eat and rest,
eat and rest.
It chews up many leaves.
It grows and grows.

Two weeks go by.
Now the caterpillar
is ready to change.
It finds a safe spot
on a twig or leaf.
It spins a silk pad.
It hangs down from the pad.

It looks as if
the caterpillar is just resting.
But it isn't!
Slowly, it sheds its skin.
Then it forms a hard shell.
Inside the shell,
the caterpillar is changing.

After about a week,
the shell cracks open.
Out comes a pretty
monarch butterfly!

Her wings are wet.
She can't fly yet.
She must let her wings
dry in the sun.

Then the monarch flies
to a bed of flowers.
She is hungry.

Butterflies do not eat leaves
like caterpillars.
They suck sweet juices
from flowers.
Their tongues work like straws.

Some animals like
to eat butterflies.
But these butterflies are safe.
Their wings look like
leaves and bark.
This bird does not see them.
Can you see them?

Are these butterflies?

No. They are moths.

Moths look a lot like butterflies.

But they fly at night.

Butterflies fly in the daytime.

Is this a butterfly?
Yes!
You can tell
because its wings
are closed.

When a moth rests,
its wings stay open.

The summer is ending.

Fall is on the way.

Most butterflies do not
like the cold.
Some sleep all winter.
They find quiet spots,
such as a cave or your attic.

Other butterflies fly south
to warm places.

Monarch butterflies
fly many, many miles.
Clouds of them fill the sky.
In the spring,
they fly back north.
There, they will lay
their eggs.

And soon,
new butterflies will be here.
Maybe some will be
in your backyard!